ADULT PIANO *Adventures®*
CLASSICS

**Arranged by
Nancy and Randall Faber**

2

Production Coordinator: Jon Ophoff
Editor: Isabel Otero Bowen
Historical Text: Marienne Uszler
Cover: Terpstra Design, San Francisco
Engraving: Dovetree Productions, Inc.

FABER
PIANO ADVENTURES®

ISBN 978-1-61677-189-8

FOREWORD

A "classic" is a work of art or literature that is recognized to be of the highest quality. Many works of art were popular in their day, but later forgotten. A classic, however, withstands the test of time and endures to be appreciated and enjoyed by later generations.

Adult Piano Adventures® Classics Book 2 celebrates the masterworks of Western music. This book is designed for those studying Adult Piano Adventures Book 2 or pianists who have reached a late elementary to early intermediate reading level. You will find appealing pianistic arrangements that can advance your skill while exploring important orchestral, keyboard, and operatic works.

This book has two main sections:

Baroque & Classical

> This first section features arrangements of outstanding masterworks from 1600 to 1830. *Baroque* music typically had a single mood throughout a piece, energetic rhythms, longer ornate melodies, and wide dynamic contrast. Baroque composers distinguished themselves with the creation of many types of music—sacred choral music, operas, and secular dance suites.

> Composers of *Classical* music responded with music that was less complex, with a lighter, clearer texture. The music was mostly homophonic—meaning the primacy of the melody to a subordinate harmony. Rhythm became clearly defined, regular, and elegant. The piano, invented by Bartolomeo Cristofori, usurped the harpsichord, leading to a keyboard revolution in the Romantic period.

Romantic & Impressionistic

> Section 2 features arrangements of magnificent treasures from the 19th and 20th centuries. *Romantic* music is characterized by expressivity and freer forms, for the orchestra and the now popular piano. These forms often had programmatic (descriptive) content, such as Grieg's *In the Hall of the Mountain King* from this collection. New harmonic colors, lyrical melodies with wider intervals, chromatic passages, and personal interpretation prevailed.

> The word "Impressionism" came from a painting by Claude Monet titled "Impression, Sunrise." This French movement embraced a fascination with tone color and the individual sound of each instrument. Fluidity of sound, thinner textures, unstable harmonies, and, above all, color and atmosphere guided Impressionistic composers.

Enjoy! May the melodies of Bach, Handel, Mozart, Beethoven, Grieg, Debussy, and many other master composers bring you meaningful musical memories.

FF3032

TABLE OF CONTENTS

BAROQUE & CLASSICAL

The first section offers late elementary to early intermediate arrangements of famous Baroque themes (1600-1750) progressing to treasured Classical themes (1750-1830).

JESU, JOY OF MAN'S DESIRING (Bach) - page 6
This famous aria comes from a cantata Bach wrote for the feast of Mary's Visitation. The aria is the closing chorale. The winding and flowing introductory music creates a relaxed and cheerful mood that supports the confident melody (M. 9). Dame Myra Hess, the great English pianist, arranged the now well-known keyboard version.

SHEEP MAY SAFELY GRAZE (Bach) - page 8
Bach provided music for the court as well as the church. This cantata was written to celebrate the birthday of Duke Christian, and it was performed in a hunting lodge. A soprano sings this aria about sheep who graze safely where a shepherd watches. The line beginning in M. 18 is the aria. The music surrounding it paints the peaceful scene.

CANON IN D (Pachelbel) - page 11
Although Pachelbel wrote mainly organ music, he composed some chamber pieces—such as the Canon and Gigue in D for three violins and ground bass. It was not published until 1919 and began its rise to popularity after a French orchestra recorded it in 1968. Your left hand needs to know only four measures of music! The ever more decorated melody winds over this ground bass. Can you trace the right-hand melody within the decorations?

RONDEAU IN D MINOR (Purcell) - page 14
The most prominent English composer of the mid-Baroque period, Henry Purcell wrote an abundance of vocal and instrumental music in the 36 years of his life. This Rondeau is the second in a set of nine string pieces written as incidental music for a play, *The Moors Revenge (Abdelazar)*, a play written by a woman, Aphra Behn. It has gained its current fame as the theme of Benjamin Britten's Young Person's Guide to the Orchestra.

PRELUDE FROM CELLO SUITE NO. 1 IN G MAJOR (Bach) - page 16
Bach was the first to write solo cello music, and he wrote six suites to provide cellists with a variety of pieces. We often think of string instruments as playing solo lines. Yet composers can create solo string music that sounds like chords! This Prelude challenges the player to sweep the bow across the strings to give that effect. Your left-hand notes need to sing out like deep, rich strings while the right hand quicker notes flow smoothly.

THE ARRIVAL OF THE QUEEN OF SHEBA (Handel) - page 20
Handel's 29 oratorios, although not staged, were as dramatic as his 42 operas. The characters and plots are often biblical. The oratorio Solomon praises how he built the Temple at Jerusalem and extended the Empire. The third act opens with the visit to his court by the Queen of Sheba. Oboes and strings play music with flourishes and pageantry.

WINTER, 3RD MOVEMENT (Vivaldi) - page 22
Vivaldi helped to define what we know as the concerto. He composed 350 for solo instrument and strings; 230 of these are for violin. Vivaldi was also a champion of program music, music that is descriptive. The concertos grouped as the "Four Seasons" had accompanying sonnets, perhaps written by Vivaldi. The "Winter" sonnet suggests "To walk on the ice with tentative steps. To slide and fall down to the ground."

SARABANDE (Handel) - page 26

The sarabande was a sung dance that began in Latin America and Spain accompanied by guitar. Later, in Europe, it became a solo instrumental piece for string or keyboard that was noted for its rhythmic pattern: triple meter with a dotted second beat. By Handel's time the sarabande was a stately dance in a set of keyboard pieces. This music is elegant!

SLEEPERS AWAKE (Bach) - page 28

Although Bach composed this cantata to be performed after Trinity, it is now usually sung during Advent. The music you play here is from the fourth chorale, *Zion Hears the Watchmen Singing*. It reflects the lilting phrases exchanged by the strings but does not include the chorale melody itself. Bach also transcribed this music as an organ solo.

THEME FROM SYMPHONY NO. 3, "EROICA" (Beethoven) - page 32

This symphony was meant to be heroic *(Eroica)*. It was dedicated to Napoleon, but when Napoleon declared himself Emperor, Beethoven scratched out that dedication. It was completely unlike any symphonies before it—a musical revolution. The fourth movement of this bold symphony is dancelike, but the dance is sturdy and steady, as well as joyous.

THEME FROM SYMPHONY NO. 40, 1ST MOVEMENT (Mozart) - page 34

Mozart used minor keys only for music that was serious or passionate. The continued use of the short phrases in the first movement provides excited energy, almost like a series of short gasps. Even when the motion is briefly interrupted (M. 17), it is with sharp accents and determined chords. This is urgent music!

AVE VERUM CORPUS (Mozart) - page 37

Mozart wrote this rather short hymn just a few months before he died for a choirmaster friend, Anton Stoll. The motet was to celebrate the feast of Corpus Christi which is why the text refers to the "true body" *(verum corpus)*. The choir is accompanied by strings and organ. All the colorful harmonies and chords must be played as smoothly as possible.

MINUET FROM DON GIOVANNI (Mozart) - page 40

Don Giovanni is one of Mozart's most famous operas. It skillfully mixes humor, tenderness, and terror to tell a dramatic story. At the close of Act 1 the Don hosts a fancy ball. There are three orchestras (two onstage, one in the pit) and each plays music for a different dance at the same time! This Minuet is the most stylish of the three.

MOONLIGHT SONATA THEME (Beethoven) - page 42

Beethoven did really suggest that this sonata was like a fantasy *(Quasi una fantasia)*, but he would not recognize it by the name we give it today. This well-known first movement sounds easy to play, but its quiet intensity is challenging to sustain. The constant triplet figure creates both a sense of mystery and serenity.

GYPSY RONDO (Haydn) - page 44

Haydn spent most of his life as the musical director in the Hungarian Esterházy Court. He would often have heard Gypsy musicians, including the dance music played by them to recruit peasants into the Austrian army. After two graceful movements, the finale of this trio explodes with fiery vigor partly because Haydn includes some of these Gypsy tunes.

PATHÉTIQUE SONATA THEME, 2ND MOVEMENT (Beethoven) - page 48

Beethoven's eighth piano sonata is the first that becomes truly intense and emotional. The dramatic first movement with its abrupt contrasts and rumbling bass tremolos gives way to this serene melodic meditation. The mood remains calm; even the quicker notes must be given time to sing. Be gentle with those descending two-note slurs! (Mm. 24-28).

Jesu, Joy of Man's Desiring

from the cantata *Herz und Mund und Tat und Leben*, BWV 147

Johann Sebastian Bach
(1685-1750)

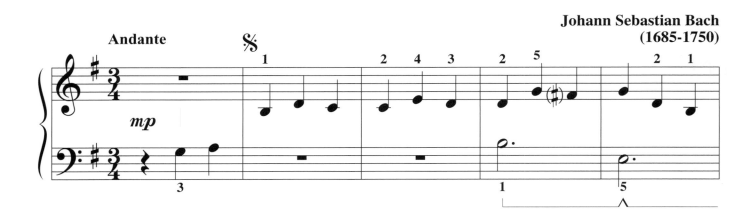

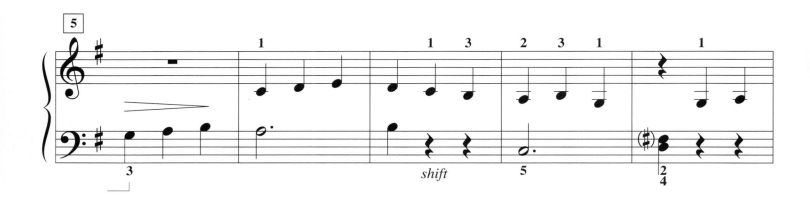

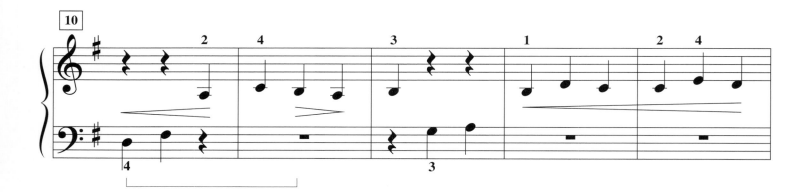

To Coda

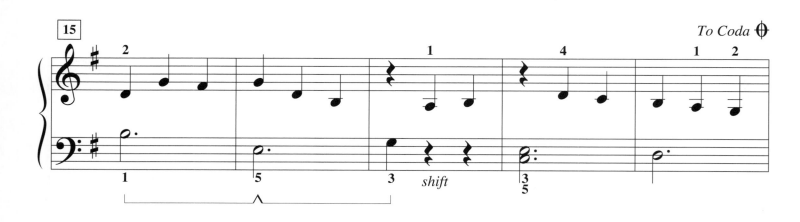

FF3032

Sheep May Safely Graze

from the cantata *Was mir behagt, ist nur die muntre Jagd*, BWV 208

Johann Sebastian Bach
(1685-1750)

FF3032

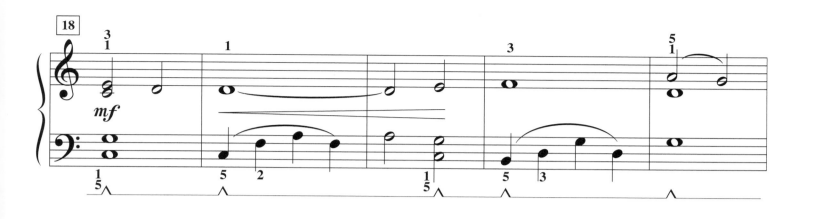

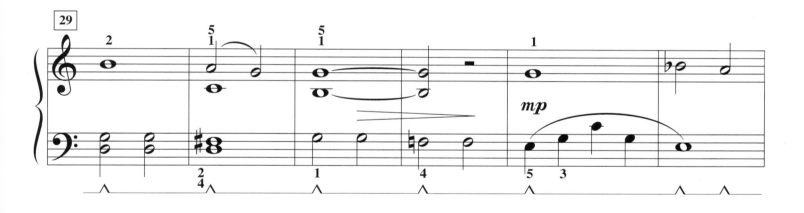

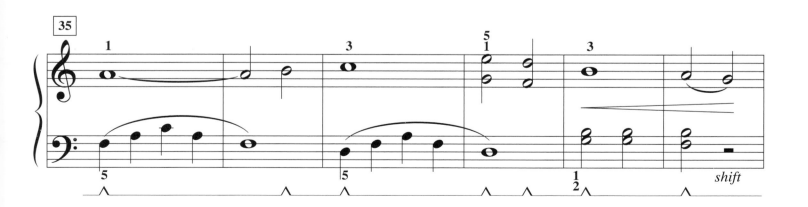

Canon in D

Johann Pachelbel
(1653-1706)

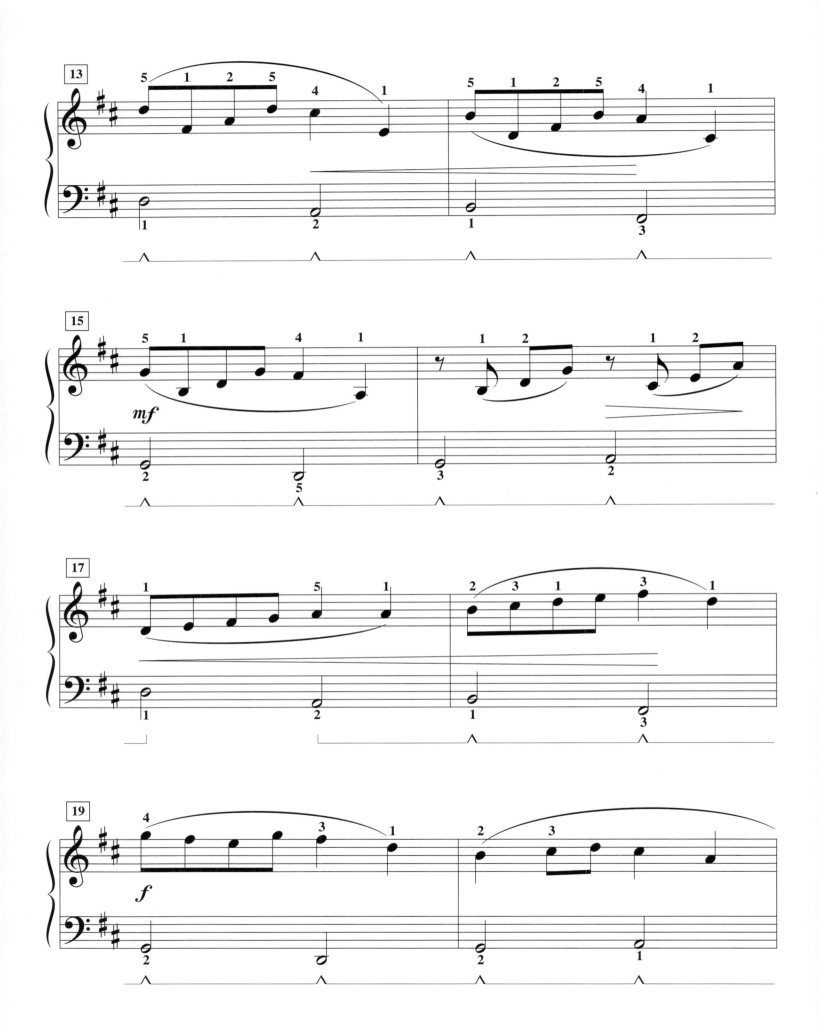

Rondeau in D Minor

from *Abdelazer,* Z. 570

Henry Purcell
(1659-1695)

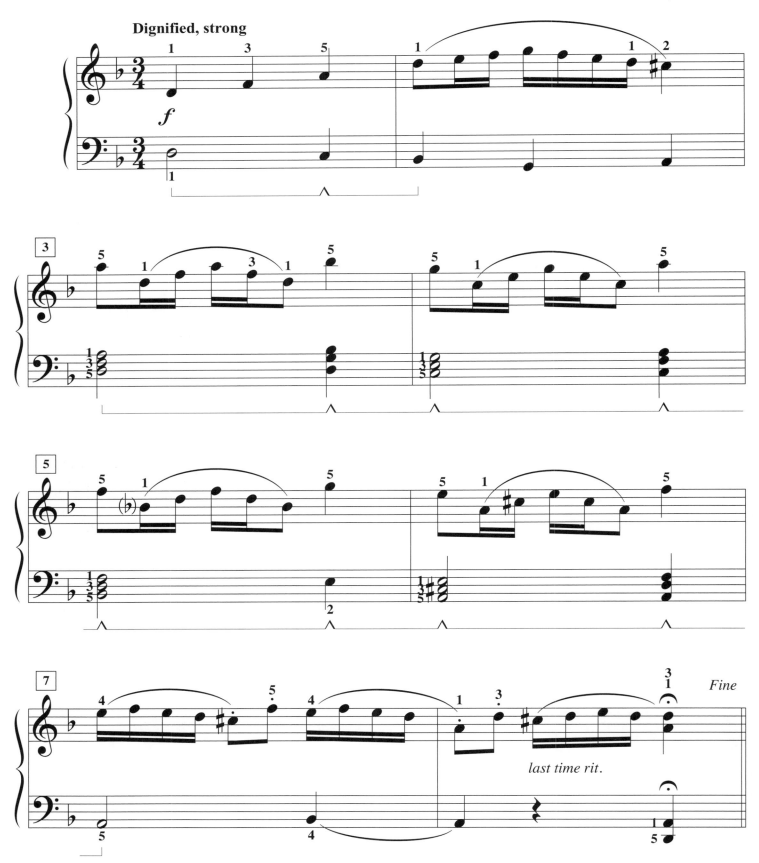

FF3032

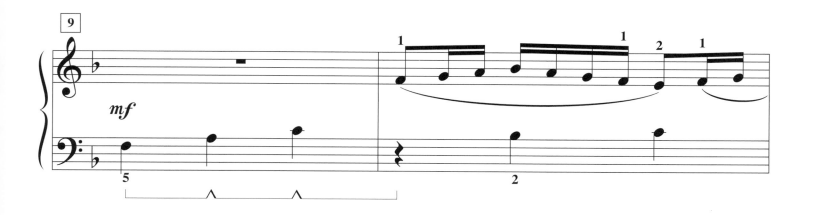

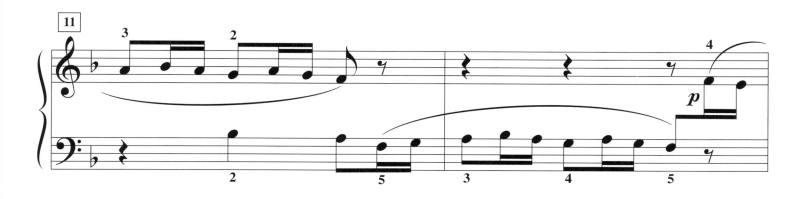

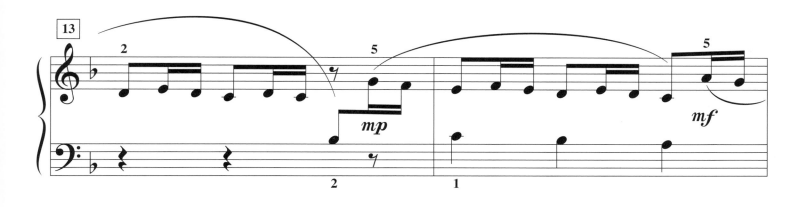

D.C. al Fine

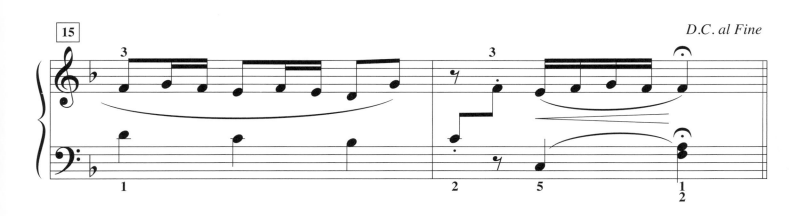

Prelude
from Cello Suite No. 1 in G Major

Johann Sebastian Bach
(1685-1750)

FF3032

The Arrival of the Queen of Sheba

from the oratorio *Solomon*, HWV 67

George Frideric Handel
(1685-1759)

Allegro

FF3032

Winter, 3rd Movement
from *The Four Seasons*

Antonio Vivaldi
(1678-1741)

FF3032

FF3032

Sarabande
from Keyboard Suite in D Minor, HWV 437

George Frideric Handel
(1685-1759)

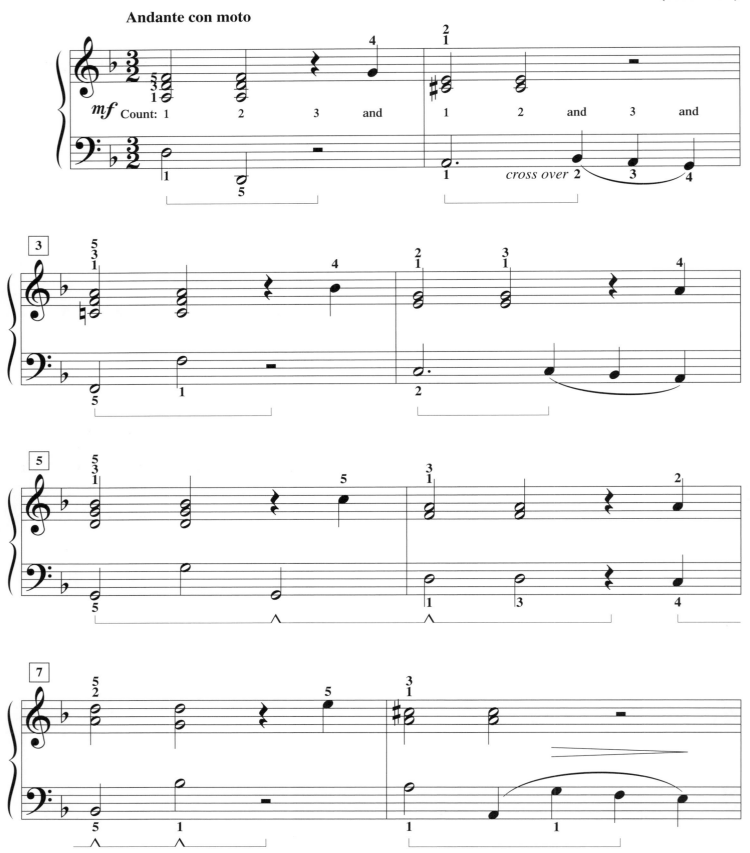

FF3032

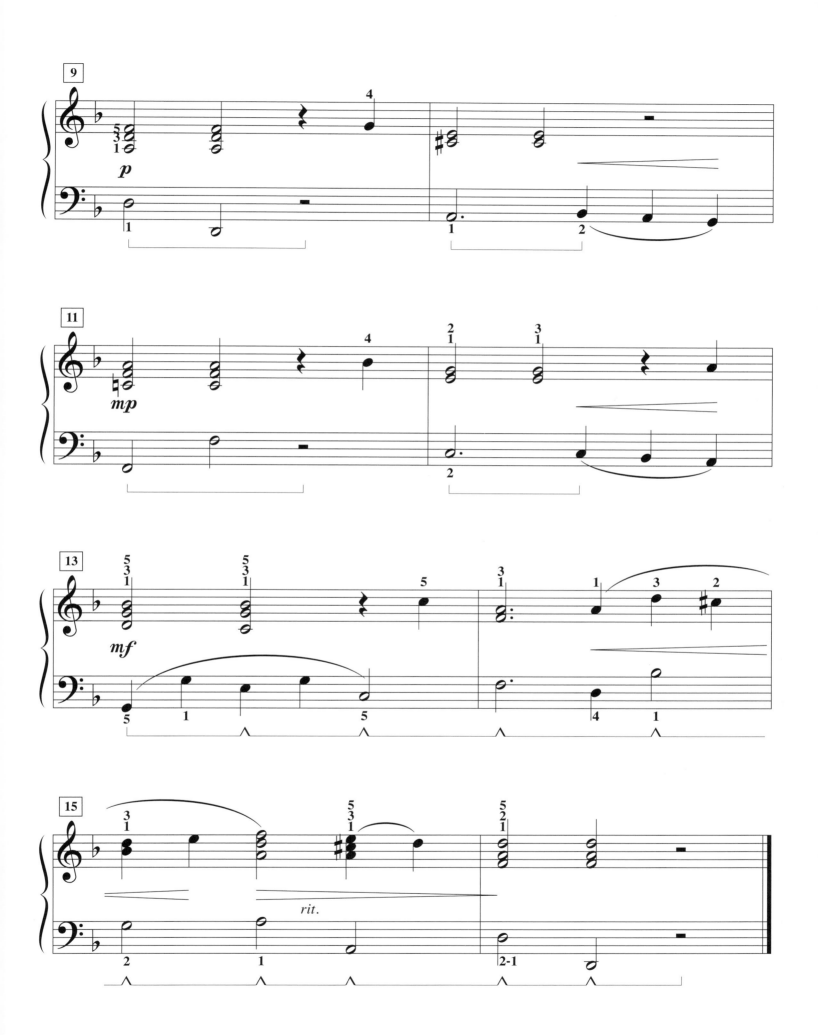

FF3032

BAROQUE

Sleepers Awake

from the chorale cantata *Wachet auf, ruft uns die Stimme*, BWV 140

Johann Sebastian Bach
(1685-1750)

FF3032

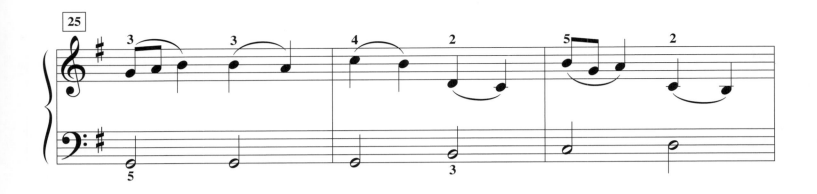

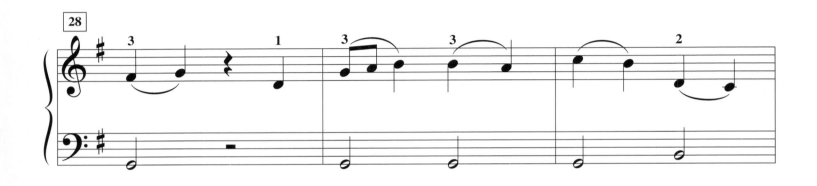

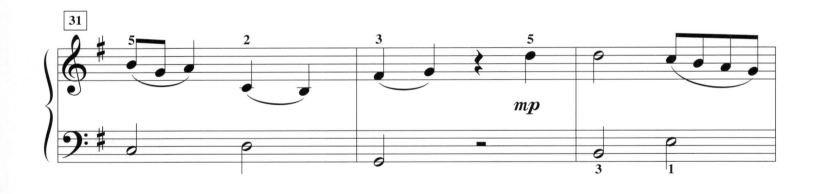

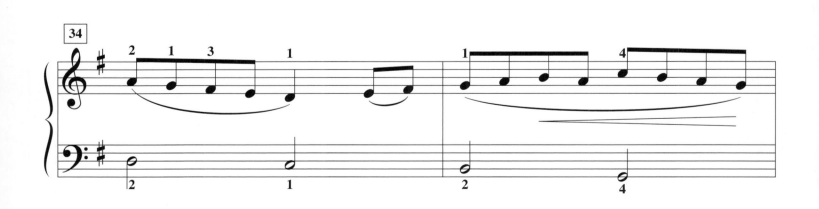

Theme from Symphony No. 3, "Eroica"

Op. 55, 4th Movement

Ludwig van Beethoven
(1770-1827)

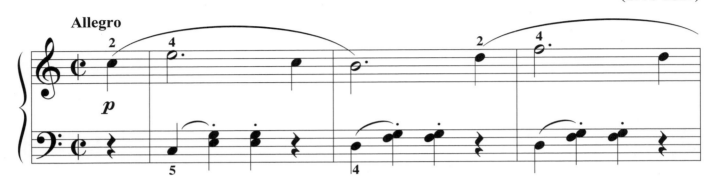

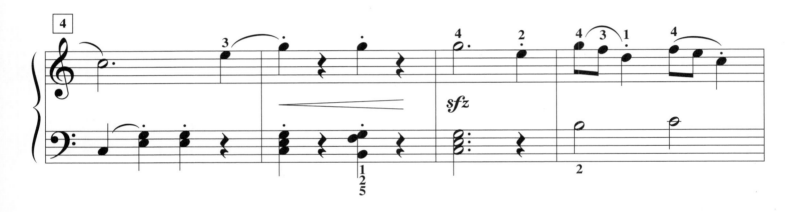

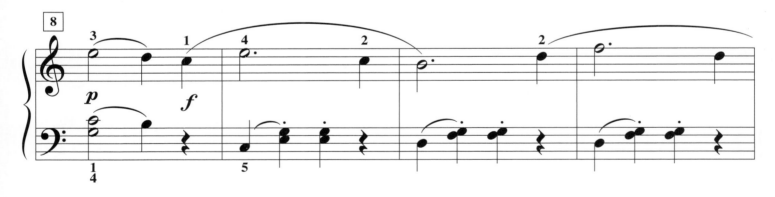

FF3032

Theme from Symphony No. 40
KV. 550, 1st Movement

Wolfgang Amadeus Mozart
(1756-1791)

FF3032

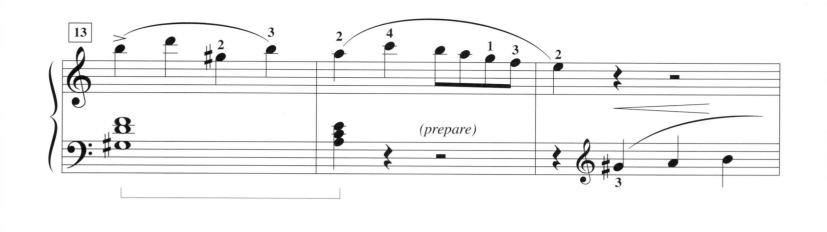

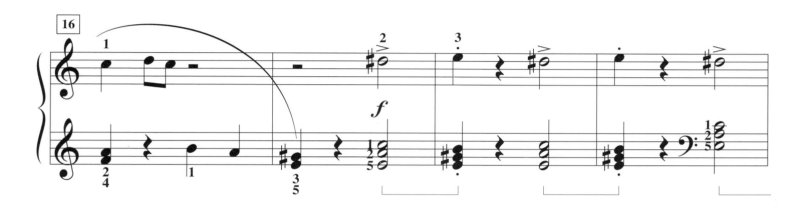

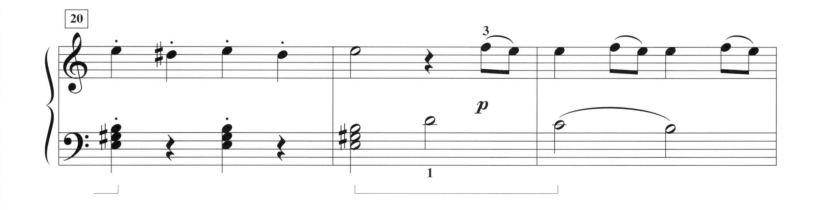

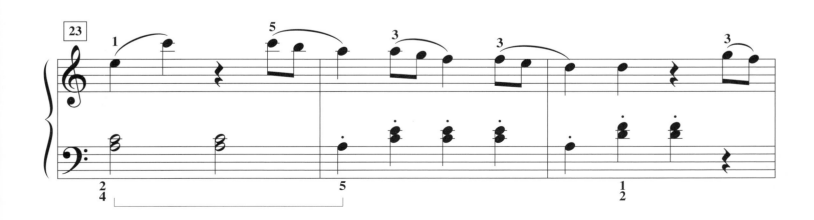

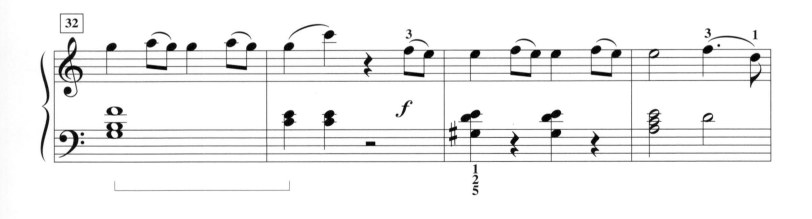

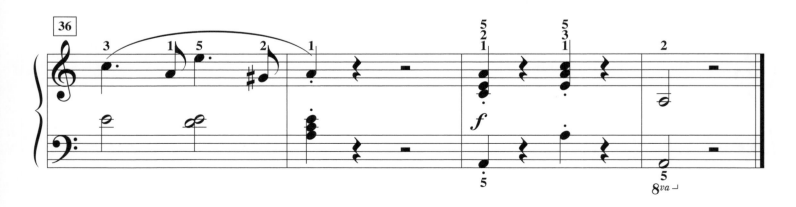

Ave Verum Corpus
Motet in D Major, K. 618

Wolfgang Amadeus Mozart
(1756-1791)

Minuet
from the opera *Don Giovanni*

Wolfgang Amadeus Mozart
(1756-1791)

FF3032

Moonlight Sonata Theme

from Piano Sonata No. 14 in C-sharp minor, *"Quasi una fantasia,"* Op. 27, No. 2

Ludwig van Beethoven
(1770-1827)

FF3032

Gypsy Rondo

from Piano Trio No. 39

Franz Joseph Haydn
(1732-1809)

FF3032

Pathétique Sonata Theme
from Piano Sonata No. 8, Op. 13, 2nd Movement

Ludwig van Beethoven
(1770-1827)

Adagio cantabile

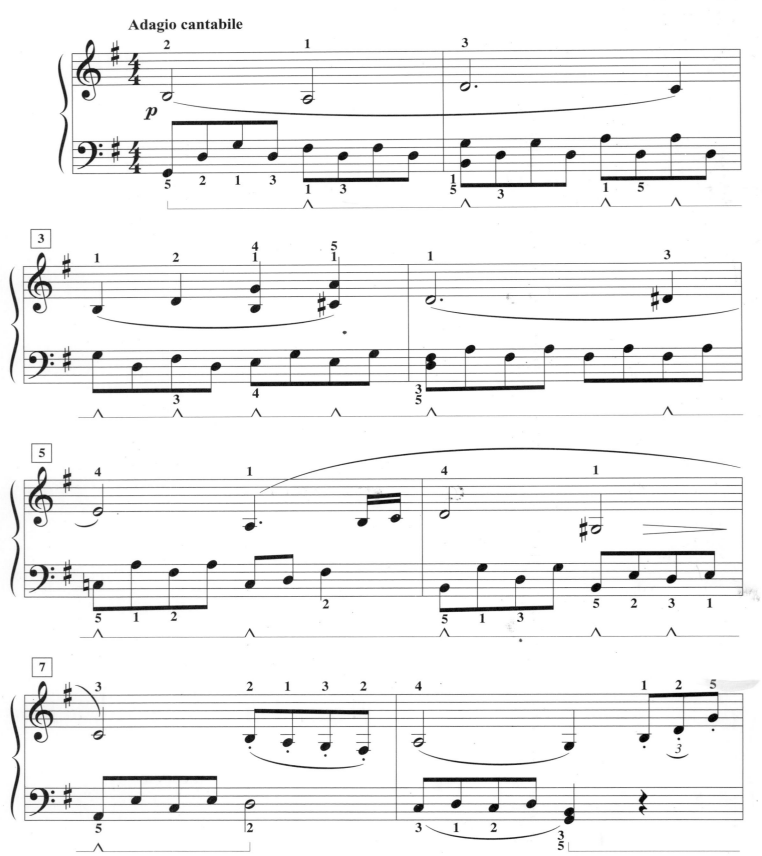

FF3032

ROMANTIC & IMPRESSIONISTIC

The second section offers late elementary to early intermediate arrangements of well-known Romantic works (approximately 1800-1850) concluding with a beloved Impressionistic theme (1870-1886).

ON WINGS OF SONG (Mendelssohn) - page 54

Like Mozart, Mendelssohn was precocious, performing and writing music fluently and easily even as a child. The son of a successful Hamburg banker, he had a broad and richly varied education. The texts he chose to set to music were often from the greatest German poets, such as this song set to a poem of Heine. Liszt transcribed this music for piano.

IN THE HALL OF THE MOUNTAIN KING (Grieg) - page 56

Grieg was invited by Henrik Ibsen, the Norwegian dramatist, to write incidental music for his new play *Peer Gynt*—a fairy tale written in poetry whose 40 scenes challenged the technical capacities of staging it. Grieg's music was played between scenes. Grieg later created two orchestral suites from these pieces and they have become some of his best-loved music. Peer is an anti-hero who travels to various continents and indulges in wild adventures. One of these is into the troll king's mountain.

MELODY IN F (Rubinstein) - page 58

As a pianist Rubinstein was a child prodigy and he toured throughout Europe, playing even for Queen Victoria. In 1862 he founded the St. Petersburg Conservatory to improve Russian music education. Tchaikovsky was his student there. He wrote in many forms throughout his life, but the *Melody in F* is his only composition that remains popular. Make sure that the left-hand harmonies enrich this simple song.

TRIUMPHAL MARCH FROM AIDA (Verdi) - page 60

Aida is one of the grandest of all "grand" operas. And the Triumphal March heard in the second act—when the hero, Radamès, returns victorious after defeating the Ethiopian army—provides for a display of spectacular pageantry, a colorful ballet, and scores of marching operatic spear-carriers! The opera exhibits the type of exoticism that gloried in foreign settings and dramatic rituals. Your right hand must ring out like resonant trumpets. Chords and rhythms must be sharp and precise. Victory!

BALLADE NO. 1 IN G MINOR (Chopin) - page 62

A ballade is a quintessential Romantic musical form, a personal and expressive narrative. Chopin is the first composer to write solo instrumental pieces using this title. His four ballades are among his masterworks. Here you play the first theme, a haunting and rather plaintive waltz. The left-hand chords must be rich, yet soft. Unlike this version, the actual Ballade ends in a storm of roaring scales and octaves.

PRELUDE OP. 28, NO. 7 (Chopin) - page 64

"Preluding" at the keyboard—improvising to demonstrate your imagination and technique—was a long-standing practice. But many performers played composed music, not trusting their improvisatory skills. Chopin's cycle of 24 Preludes can be seen in this light. There is a piece in each major and minor key that offers a variety of moods and pianistic effects. This is the shortest of the preludes, a simple series of graceful phrases.

HUMORESQUE (Dvořák) - page 65

Dvořák spent three years at what was then the National Conservatory of Music in New York City. He was interested in what he regarded as "American music," the music of native Americans and African-Americans. Inspired by this music he wrote the Symphony "From the New World." This piece is from a group of eight piano Humoresques written after his return to Bohemia. He later arranged these for many instrumental combinations.

SERENADE (Schubert) - page 68

This *Serenade* is one of fourteen in the last group of songs Schubert wrote and, because of that, the publisher issued these as his "Swan Song" *(Schwanengesang)* after he died. Liszt later wrote a piano transcription of this song. A serenade is often accompanied by guitar, and you can imagine your left hand plucking and strumming while the right hand sings. Is this a sad or hopeful serenade? By the frequent changes from minor to major Schubert makes you wonder.

YOU AND YOU (Strauss, Jr.) - page 71

The Strauss family were musicians who wrote and played Viennese dance music, but it was Johann, Jr. who became the Waltz King. His waltzes were no longer "beer-garden dances," but more sophisticated music mirroring the gaiety of 19th-century imperial Vienna. In addition to a multitude of waltzes and polkas, he also wrote a number of operettas, the most famous of which is *Die Fledermaus*. He conducted the orchestra with his violin, standing and walking among the players. This, like many of his waltzes, is really a string of melodies, each more high-spirited and lilting.

CLAIR DE LUNE (Debussy) - page 74

Debussy had an affinity with the French Symbolist movement and its evocation of the indefinite. In his music he spoke of using "floating chords." *Clair de lune* is the third in a set of four pieces grouped under a title drawn from a poem by Paul Verlaine. In his poem Verlaine refers to dancing "masqueraders and bergamaskers," a possible reason for the title *Suite bergamasque*. The second and fourth pieces in the suite are dances, but this piece depicts the filmy moonlight in which the dancers are swaying. Good use of the pedal will help you create an elegant dream.

On Wings of Song

from *Six Songs for Voice and Piano*, Op. 34

Felix Mendelssohn
(1809-1847)

FF3032

In the Hall of the Mountain King

from *Peer Gynt*, Op. 23

Edvard Grieg
(1843-1907)

FF3032

Melody in F
Op. 3, No. 1

Anton Rubinstein
(1829-1894)

Moderato, cantabile

FF3032

Triumphal March
from the opera *Aida*

Giuseppe Verdi
(1813-1901)

FF3032

Ballade
No. 1 in G Minor, Op. 23

Frédéric Chopin
(1810-1849)

FF3032

Prelude
Op. 28, No. 7

Frédéric Chopin
(1810-1849)

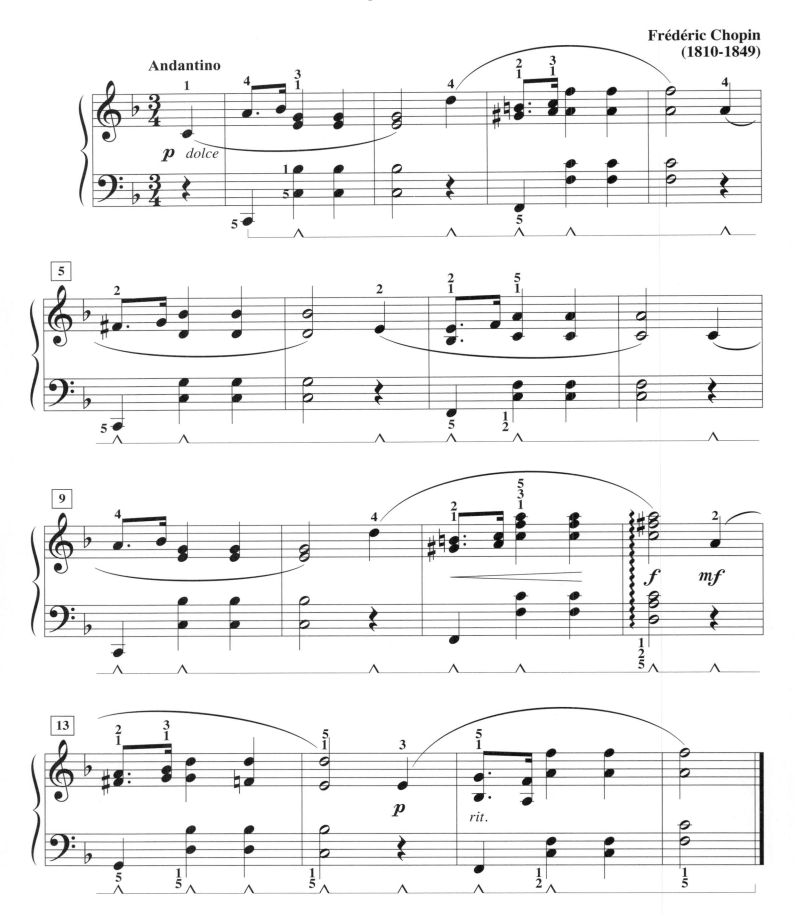

FF303

Humoresque

No. 7 from 8 *Humoresques*, Op. 101

Antonín Dvořák
(1841-1904)

Andante grazioso

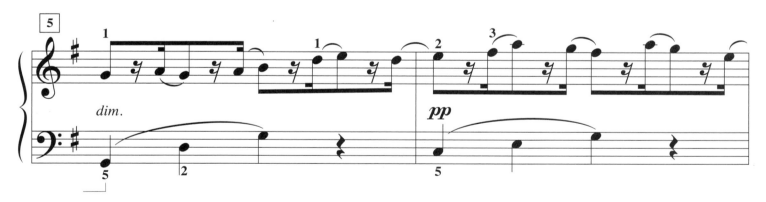

FF3032

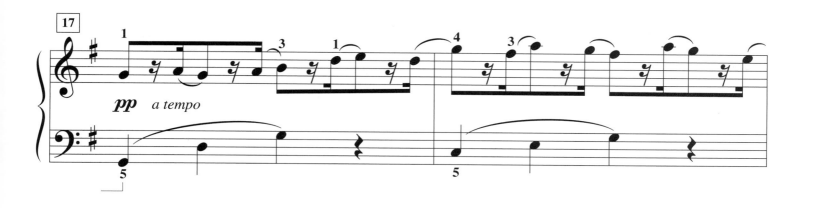

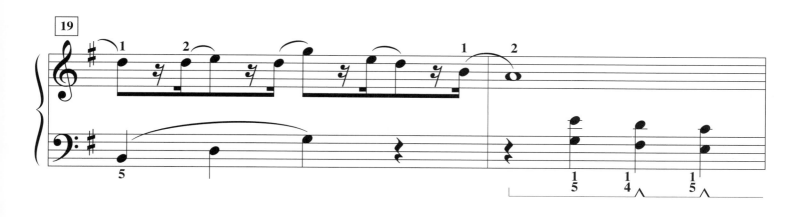

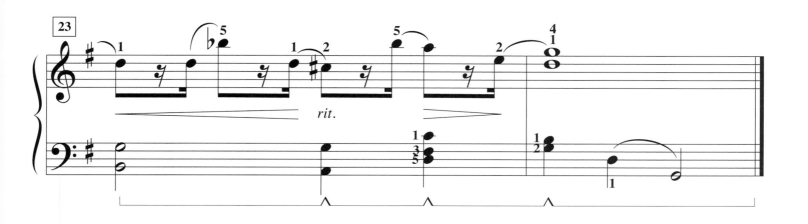

Serenade
from *Schwanengesang*, D.957

Franz Schubert
(1797-1828)

FF303

You and You

from the opera *Die Fledermaus*, Op. 367

Johann Strauss, Jr.
(1825-1899)

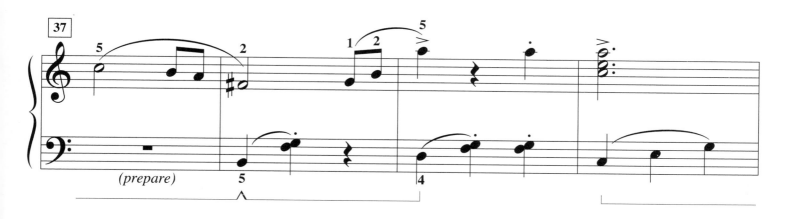

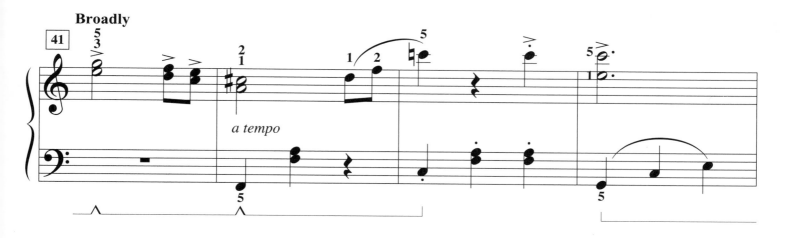

Clair de lune
from *Suite bergamasque,* 3rd Movement

Claude Debussy
(1862-1918)

FF30

DICTIONARY OF MUSICAL TERMS

DYNAMIC MARKS

pp	***p***	***mp***	***mf***	***f***	***ff***
pianissimo very soft	*piano* soft	*mezzo piano* moderately soft	*mezzo forte* moderately loud	*forte* loud	*fortissimo* very loud

crescendo (cresc.)
Play gradually louder.

diminuendo (dim.) or decrescendo (decresc.)
Play gradually softer.

TEMPO MARKS

Adagio	***Andante***	***Moderato***	***Allegretto***	***Allegro***
slowly	walking speed	moderate speed	rather fast	fast

SIGN	TERM	DEFINITION
	accent mark	Play this note louder.
	a tempo	Return to the original tempo (speed).
BWV	***Bach-Werke-Verzeichnis***	The catalog of the complete works of Johann Sebastian Bach.
	cantabile	Singing.
	cantata	A vocal musical work based on a text, usually with several movements.
	concerto	A composition for a solo instrument and orchestra.
	con moto	With motion.
¢	**cut time (alla breve)**	$\frac{2}{2}$ time. The half note receives the beat (two half-note beats per measure).
D.C. al Fine	***Da Capo al Fine***	Return to the beginning and play until *Fine* (end).
D.S. al Coda	***Dal Segno al Coda***	Return to the 𝄋 sign and play to ⊕, then jump to the *Coda*.
D.S. al Fine	***Dal Segno al Fine***	Return to the 𝄋 sign and play until *Fine* (end).
	damper pedal	The right pedal, which sustains the sound, played with the right foot.
	dotted quarter note	A dot adds half the value to the note. A dotted quarter is the equivalent of a quarter note tied to an eighth note.
	e	And (Italian). For example *cresc. e rit.*
	eighth rest	Silence for the value of an eighth note.
	fermata	Hold this note longer than its normal value.
1. 2.	**1st and 2nd endings**	Play the 1st ending and repeat from the beginning. Then play the 2nd ending, skipping over the 1st ending.
	Fine	End here.
	grace note	An ornamental note that is played quickly into the note that follows.
	humoresque	A humorous story or sketch.
	ledger line	A short line used to extend the staff.
	legato	Smooth, connected.
	maestoso	Majestic, stately.

	minuet	An elegant dance in $\frac{3}{4}$ time. The dance was popular in the 1700s.
	molto	Very. For example, *molto rit.* means to make a big *ritard*.
	motet	A short vocal composition, often on a sacred text.
	opera	A drama set to music, with singing, acting, and sometimes, dancing. In an opera, the characters express themselves by singing instead of speaking.
Op.	**opus**	Work. A composer's compositions are often arranged in sequence. Each major work is given an opus number.
	oratorio	A major composition based on a religious text which may include vocal solos, choruses, instrumental ensembles, and a narrator.
8va	*ottava*	Play one octave higher (or lower) than written.
	pedal change	Shows the up-down motion of the damper pedal.
	poco a poco	Little by little.
rall.	*rallentando*	Gradually slowing down. Same as *ritardando*.
	religioso	Reverent, solemn.
‖: :‖	**repeat sign**	Play the music within the repeat signs again.
rit.	*ritardando*	Gradually slowing down.
	rolled chord	Play the notes one at a time, rapidly, from bottom to top.
	sarabande	A stately Baroque dance in slow triple time.
	sempre	Always. For example, *sempre staccato* means to continue playing staccato.
sfz	*sforzando*	A sudden, strong accent.
	simile	Similarly. Continue in the same way (same pedaling, same use of staccato, etc.).
	sixteenth notes	Four sixteenth notes equal one quarter note.
	sixteenth rest	Silence for the value of a sixteenth note.
	slur	A curved line that indicates legato playing.
	sonata	An instrumental piece, often with 3 movements.
	staccato	Detached, disconnected.
sub.	*subito*	Suddenly. For example, *subito piano* means suddenly soft.
	suite	A set of short pieces, often written in dance forms.
	symphony	A major composition for orchestra. A symphony has several sections called movements (ususally four).
	tempo di valse	Waltz tempo.
	tenuto mark	Hold the note for its full value. Stress by pressing gently into the key.
	theme	The main melody of a composition. (Many works have more than one theme.)
	tie	A curved line that connects two notes on the same line or space. Hold for the total counts of both notes.
tr	**trill**	A quick repetition of the principle note with the note above it.
	triplet	Three eighth notes to a quarter note.
	waltz	A popular 19th century dance in $\frac{3}{4}$ time.

COMPOSER INDEX